How to Draw Harry Potter 1

The Step-by-Step Harry Potter Drawing Book

By

David K.

License Notes

No part of this Book can be reproduced in any form or by any means including print, electronic, scanning or photocopying unless prior permission is granted by the author.

All ideas, suggestions and guidelines mentioned here are written for informative purposes. While the author has taken every possible step to ensure accuracy, all readers are advised to follow information at their own risk. The author cannot be held responsible for personal and/or commercial damages in case of misinterpreting and misunderstanding any part of this Book

Table of Contents

Introduction

The sky's the limit when it comes to drawing. We are confident that by consulting our educational book, you will be well on your way to becoming a drawing expert!

Children, listen up: we know how smart you are, and we're convinced that you'll quickly learn the principles explained in this manual.

Please remember that drawing – just like painting, playing a musical instrument, or joining a soccer team – requires one key element: practice.

That's right, be patient with yourselves, kids. No one learned to draw a complex cartoon character or firetruck overnight! But the more you consult this book and stick with our tips and drawing techniques, the more you will see your artistic skills improving.

Parents, be supportive and offer constructive criticism to your young creators. After all, how neat would it be to receive your next birthday card with an awesome drawing from your kid?

Drawing can be a wonderful bonding experience between parents and their children. Kids often express themselves better through images rather than words, so listen to what they have to say when looking at their creations and ask questions when appropriate.

Don't wait any longer – add this incredible book to your collection and enjoy every minute of your time spent as a family!

How to Draw Harry Potter

Step 1.

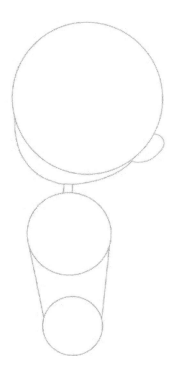

Draw circle for the head and add his jaw, and ear.
Add a circle for the chest, and a circle for the hips.
Connect them to make the body.

Step 2.

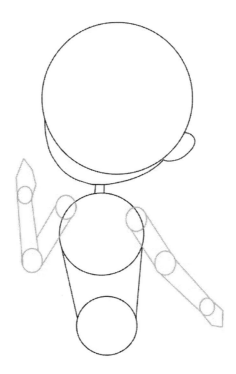

Add a three circles to each side.
One for the shoulder, one for the elbow and one
for the wrist.

Connect them to make the arms and add the
outline of the hand.

Step 3.

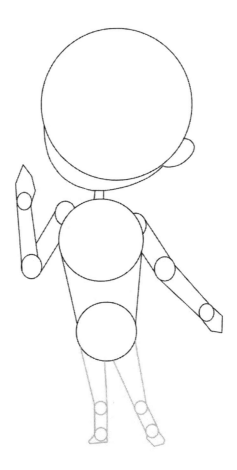

Add four circles underneath the hips.
Two for the knees and two for the ankles.

Connect them to make the legs and draw the outline of the feet.

Step 4.

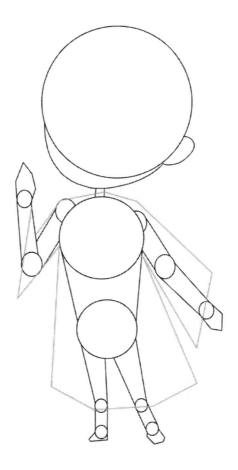

Draw the outline of his wizard robe around his body.

Make sure to draw the sleeves wide and big to give it an extra magical feel.

Step 5.

Add the outline of his scarf around
his neck.

Step 6.

Go back to head and draw his big puffy hair around it.

Use the example to help you along.

Step 7.

Redraw his face by adding the inside of
his ear, his eyebrows, glasses, eyes, nose and
mouth.

Step 8.

Redraw the scarf and divide it into separate
squares as in the example.

Step 9.

Redraw his robe and add the collar to it.
Draw the collar of his shirt and

add the tie. Separate the tie into small
squares as well.
Make his sleeves more curved to give
it volume.

Step 10.

Redraw his hands as in the example and add a
wand
to his right hand.

Then, redraw the pants to give it cuffs and add his
boots.

Step 11.

All done! Time to color!

Step 12.

His hair is dark brown and his skin
is light orange.
His scarf and tie are red with yellow.

The collar of his shirt is white and the collar of his robe is red.

His pants, boots and robe are dark gray, and his wand is light brown.

Step 13.

Add some color to give it more volume!

Step 14.

Colored version.

Step 15.

Line art version.

How to Draw Hermione

Step 1.

Draw circle for the head and add her jaw, and ear.
Add a circle for the chest, and a circle for the hips.
Connect them to make the body.

Step 2.

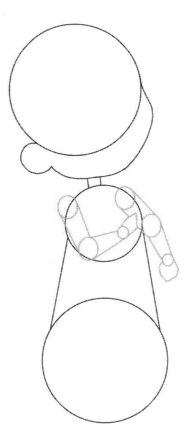

Add a three circles to each side.

One for the shoulder, one for the elbow and one for the wrist.

Connect them to make the arms and add the outline of the hand.

Step 3.

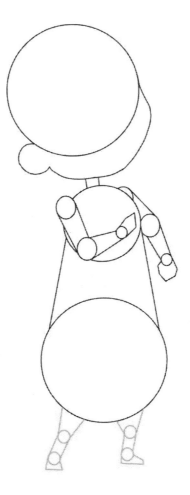

Add four circles underneath the hips.
Two for the knees and two for the ankles.
Connect them to make the legs and draw the
outline of the feet.

Step 4.

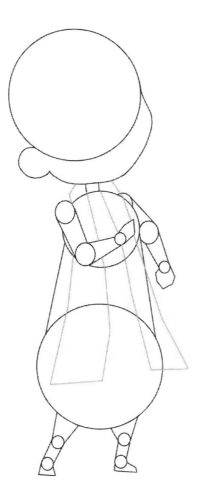

Add the outline of her scarf around
her neck.

Step 5.

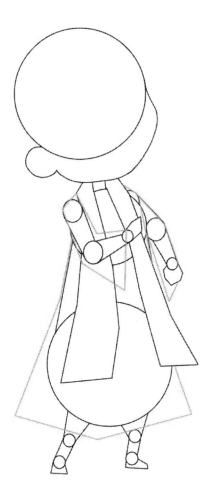

Draw the outline of her wizard robe around her body.

Make sure to draw the sleeves wide and big to give it an extra magical feel.

Step 6.

Go back to head and draw her long, puffy hair around it.

Use the example to help you along.

Step 7.

Redraw her face by adding the inside of her ear, her eyebrows, eyes with eyelashes, nose and mouth.

Make her eyelashes big as in the example.
Her lips are nice and full.

Step 8.

Redraw the scarf and divide it into separate
squares as
in the example.

Step 9.

Redraw her robe and add the collar to it.

Draw the collar of her shirt and add the tie.
Separate the tie into small squares
as well.
Make her sleeves more curved to give
it volume.
Redraw her hands as in the example.

Step 10.

Add a wand to her right hand.
Then, redraw the pants to give it cuffs and add her
boots.

Step 11.

All done! Time to color!

Step 12.

Her hair is dark brown and her skin is light orange.
Her scarf and tie are red with yellow.

The collar of her shirt is white and the collar of her robe is red.

Her pants, boots and robe are dark gray, and her wand is light brown.

Step 13.

Add some color to give it more volume!

Step 14.

Colored version.

Step 15.

Line art version.

How to Draw Ron

Step 1.

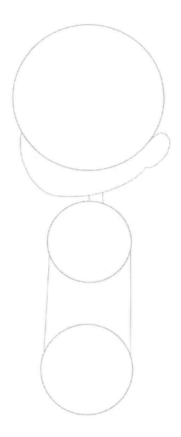

Draw circle for the head and add his jaw, and ear.
Add a circle for the chest, and a circle
for the hips.

Connect them to make the body.

Step 2.

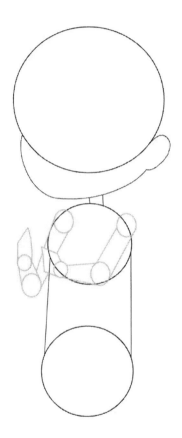

Add a three circles to each side, and make sure his hands are facing forward.

One for the shoulder, one for the elbow and one for the wrist.

Connect them to make the arms and add the outline of the hand.

Step 3.

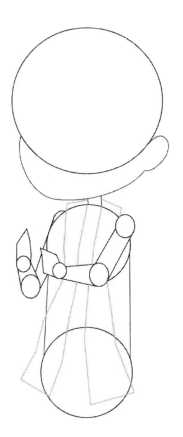

Add the outline of his scarf around
his neck.

Step 4.

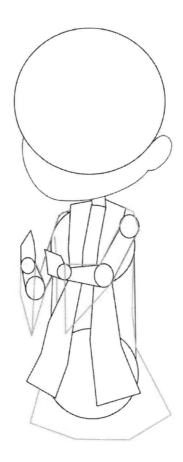

Draw the outline of his wizard robe around his body.

Make sure to draw the sleeves wide and big to give it an extra magical feel.

Step 5.

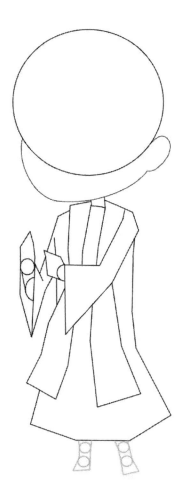

Add four circles underneath the hips.
Two for the knees and two for the ankles.

Connect them to make the legs and draw the outline of the feet.

Step 6.

Go back to head and draw his big puffy hair
around it.
See how it covers most of his forehead=

Use the example to help you along.

Step 7.

Redraw his face by adding the inside of his ear, his eyes, nose and mouth.

Step 8.

Redraw the scarf.

Step 9.

Redraw his robe and add the collar to it.

Draw the collar of his shirt and add the tie.

Separate the tie into small squares

as well.
Make his sleeves more curved to give
it volume.

Step 10.

Divide the scarf into separate squares as in the example

Redraw his hands as in the example and add a
wand
to his right hand.
Then, redraw the pants to give it cuffs and add his
boots.

Step 11.

Add the wand to his left hand.

Step 12.

All done! Time to color!

Step 13.

His hair is dark brown and his skin is
light orange.

His scarf and tie are red with yellow.
The collar of his shirt is white and the collar of his robe is red.
His pants, boots and robe are dark gray, and his wand is light brown.

Step 14.

Add some color to give it more volume!

Step 15.

Colored version.

Step 16.

Line art version

About the Author

David K.

How to draw books can be a family affair and this is the approach I wanted to take when I wrote the book. You can apply my principles to any type work you might be interested in creating in the future. With that said, let's talk a little about me and my background, so you can understand what drove me to be passionate about drawing.

My name is David K, and I voluntarily decided to leave my last name off, and use only the first initial. You might wonder why and think it is slightly secretive. Perhaps, it is a little. But I don't want anyone to concentrate on my origin, my background or nationality. This is about creating images, drawing, and not about cultural differences.

However, I can tell you this about me: since I can remember, I always loved to draw and decide to take this passion to the next level when I was in my mid-twenties. Please join me in my journey. My inspiration always been the people and things I am surrounded with. Sure, I have used my imagination and created fantastic characters, unrealistic objects and environments, but I prefer to concentrate my drawings on anything that is close to my heart. I asked friends of mine to help write about drawing methods and advice. I will also share with my readers their expertise on how to draw a book. This will be an excellent reference tool for you. People all have so many different ways to express themselves through drawings and it will definitely be beneficial and fun to learn about my friend's unique styles, I promise!

Made in the USA
Columbia, SC
17 December 2018